SHORTSTOP

THE
WINNING
EDGE

SHORTSTOP

By BOB CLUCK
Foreword by GARRY TEMPLETON

CONTEMPORARY
BOOKS, INC.
CHICAGO • NEW YORK

Library of Congress Cataloging-in-Publication Data

Cluck, Bob.
  The winning edge : shortstop.

  1. Shortstop (Baseball)—Juvenile literature.
I. Title.
GV870.5.C55   1987   796.357'24   86-32911
ISBN 0-8092-4785-2 (pbk.)

Diagrams from *The Complete Book of Baseball
Instruction* by Dell Bethel; used with permission
of Contemporary Books.
All photos courtesy Teri Cluck Photography
Equipment courtesy San Diego School of Baseball

Published by Contemporary Books, Inc.
180 North Michigan Avenue, Chicago, Illinois 60601
Manufactured in the United States of America
Library of Congress Catalog Card Number: 86-32911
International Standard Book Number: 0-8092-4785-2

Published simultaneously in Canada by Beaverbooks, Ltd.
195 Allstate Parkway, Valleywood Business Park
Markham, Ontario L3R 4T8 Canada

To Teri, Jennifer, and Amber
for patience during the long road trips
and the film sessions at home
over 20 great years

Contents

Foreword

I've been playing baseball since I was eight years old, when I began with Little League. My father was the one who taught me how to see the ball and stop it the best I could. I remember him telling me that, eventually, I would learn my range and develop my throwing from different angles. And he told me that, as a hitter, it was most important to make contact with the ball, as opposed to trying to hit it out of the park every time I was at bat.

Baseball has always been my first love, but it wasn't until I began going to big league games that I realized I wanted to be a professional ballplayer. I'm sure that the fundamentals I learned as a kid and the hard practice I put in made it easier for me to break into the majors.

Being a good shortstop takes a lot more than learning how to field a ball. Aside from the physical talents, the mental part of the game is what separates the average shortstop from the great shortstop. You must be prepared mentally to know when and where to throw the ball in hundreds of situations. It's up to you to know the basics of the game and the fine points of the shortstop position, so that you can decide—in the blink of an eye— where to throw that ball.

Of course, this does not mean you should storm onto the field like a tornado, diving and twisting all over. It means you have to learn what your capabilities are, improve on the ones that need some work, and remember that everyone—even the pros—have to practice. I've had many, many coaches, and, while many of them have had their own ways of teaching, they all agree on one thing: you have to be the best you can be. Don't try to play just like your teammate, just try to be yourself.

Be relaxed in the field, concentrate, and have patience. This book will help you to understand those all-important fundamentals you need to know to be a winner. Work hard, and you'll be on your way to becoming your best as a shortstop and as an athlete.

Garry Templeton
San Diego Padres

1
General Infield Play and Positioning

USE THE PROPER GLOVE

Most young middle infielders use a glove that is too big for them and so they have trouble handling the ball cleanly. A glove is something you cannot "grow into," and if you use a big glove in the infield, you'll always have trouble getting the ball out of the glove.

The proper glove for an infielder is small, light, and flexible.

11

POSITIONING FOR THE SHORTSTOP

You should start at medium depth (about halfway back on the dirt), and adjust from there depending on the hitter. If the hitter pulls the ball a lot or hits it up the middle, you would obviously shade him that way. When the hitter is a fast runner, logic tells you that you should play in to have a chance to throw him out. When a coach aligns the defense with the infield "in," he wants all the infielders to play on the edge of the grass. The shortstop must also adjust to each game situation. You should know the number of outs, and certainly what each base runner run might represent. An alert shortstop should be aware of each runner's speed and his tendencies as a base stealer.

THE INITIAL POSITION

The initial position is a relaxed position in which you are anticipating the next play. The better shortstops want every ball to be hit to them. The shortstop is often not only the smartest player on the field but the most gifted athlete. Your hands can be on your knees at this point, and you should be checking the base runners, opposing coaches, and hitter for any sign that might tip their offensive plans. Watch your coach, the pitcher, and the catcher in case someone is putting on a bunt or pickoff sign.

As the shortstop you are the field coordinator for the defense and will often be the guy responsible for moving the outfielders according to the coach's or manager's wishes. It is a good idea for you (and the second baseman) to know the signs the catcher gives the pitcher. If an off-speed pitch is coming, you might lean a little in the hole (to your right) and be able to make a play that would have been impossible. Infielders must remember not to move physically, because the hitter will see the movement toward the hole and know what pitch is coming. There have been cases of shortstops moving early and giving away the pitches for a whole game, causing a pitcher with good stuff to get bombed.

SHORTSTOP

Keep your feet a little more than shoulder-width apart, with your hands either on your knees or hanging relaxed. When you assume this position, all of the "homework" (number of outs, runners' positions, etc.) has already been done.

Think about the game situation while in your initial position.

THE READY POSITION

When the pitcher begins his windup, you switch from the initial position to the "ready" position. The ready position is similar to a basketball player guarding another, or a defensive back or linebacker poised for the snap. You are relaxed but ready to break in any direction at the crack of the bat. As the pitch approaches the hitting area, most shortstops take two small steps forward to put the body in motion, allowing for a quicker start. Or it might appear as a little jump. At any rate, you should not start from a "dead stop."

Assume the ready position when the pitcher starts his windup.

FIELDING THE BALL

You must get used to charging most balls hit to you. Many of the throws are long, and by charging the ball you will cut down the distance. As you approach the ball, "break down" your body (cut down your speed) and use what might be called the "four-count movement."

Your glove should be wide open as the ball approaches it. You must open it, for it won't get to this position by itself. Expect the ball to stay down, because you can react much quicker coming up should the ball take a big hop.

Your right foot (for right-handed players) is used to change gears and slow down as you approach the ball. Your left foot continues this process and contributes to overall balance and stability. If time allows (if you charge the ball there should be time), a second set of movements called a "crow hop" will prepare you to throw. Plant your right foot for the pushoff and step in the direction of the throw with your left foot. Transfer your weight smoothly from right foot to left as you release the ball.

The "mouth" of your glove must be open to receive the ball, and you should stay down and expect the ball to stay low.

*With a "half glove," you will have to be perfect
and will usually mishandle too many grounders.*

Use your right foot to slow down after charging the ball aggressively.

Your left foot follows and gets your body under control.

Plant your right foot for the throw.

As your left foot comes down in the direction of the throw, your weight is transferred from back to front.

THROWING WITH ARM STRENGTH AND ACCURACY

Whenever possible, hold the ball across the seams when throwing. While playing catch, you can learn to find the seam quite easily. After considerable practice, you will automatically throw across the seams in a game situation. Even if you don't always attain the perfect grip, you'll notice gradual improvement. Don't watch the flight of the ball as it crosses the diamond; watch the target all the way.

As you set up to throw, your front side must rotate closed (left shoulder across the body) for maximum leverage. This simple movement will provide all the power necessary to make a firm throw. If you throw too hard, your mechanics will break down and a throwing error will probably result.

Throw overhand whenever possible.

Accuracy is a combination of athletic ability, concentration, and practice.

The cross-seam grip provides the greatest accuracy and carry on your throw.

The overhand throw is recommended for almost all throws that a shortstop must make.

25

TO BE A GOOD SHORTSTOP, REMEMBER

▶ Use a glove that is small enough to handle the ball easily.
▶ Be alert and know the game situation at all times.
▶ Know the hitters and position yourself and your teammates accordingly.
▶ Assume the "ready" position on every pitch.
▶ Charge nearly every ball.
▶ In order to make accurate throws you must use a "cross-seam" grip and practice hard.

2
Slow Hit Balls and Balls Hit to the Sides

SLOW HIT BALLS

When you assume a good ready position, you can break quickly in any direction. Slow hit balls present a special problem in that you must charge through the ball and never really set yourself to throw. Whenever possible, field the ball with two hands "off" the left foot (when the left foot comes down), transfer the ball from glove to hand, and throw when the right foot comes down.

Charge the slow hit ball and field it when your left foot comes down.

Slow Hit Balls and Balls Hit to the Sides

Field the ball with both hands in front of your body and transfer the ball quickly to your throwing hand.

When your right foot comes down again, make the throw with an underhand flip.

BALLS HIT UP THE MIDDLE

The ball hit hard up the middle is a fairly difficult play. If you have to extend for the ball, it is difficult to get any velocity on the throw. Most shortstops just try to get rid of the ball quickly and don't worry about the velocity.

The ball up the middle that bounces slowly over the mound is a little easier because the shortstop is heading toward his target (first base) as he throws.

BALLS HIT IN THE HOLE

Many baseball experts believe that the ground ball in the hole is the play that separates the average shortstop from the good one. When a ball is hit to your right you must first establish the shortest angle you can take to the ball. After you have the angle, try to get in front of the ball. The only time you should backhand the ball is when you can't get in front of it. Too many infielders take it easy going after some balls and backhand unnecessarily.

If the ball is a backhand play, grab it as your left foot is coming down, if possible. Then plant your right foot and use it to push off with. With all of your momentum going away from the target, it is possible that you will need an extra step or two to get under control before you throw.

31

On a backhand play catch the ball as your left foot comes down, if at all possible.

Plant your right foot and use it to push off to get the most on the throw.

3
The Double Play

THE 6-4-3 DOUBLE PLAY

The execution of the double play begins with good positioning. If the shortstop and second baseman are at good double-play depth, most DPs are easily executed.

When you begin the double play, you do it in one of two ways. If the ball is hit to your left (toward the bag), you will use an underhand flip to the second baseman. After catching the ball, get it out of your glove so the second baseman can see it clearly, and then flip the ball chest high to him. If the ball is hit to your right, use an overhand throw after planting your right foot.

When the ball is hit near the bag (within two steps), it is faster for you to make the play yourself.

35

On ground balls near the bag, field the ball, take it out of your glove, and flip it chest high to the second baseman.

When the ball is hit toward the hole (to your right), plant your right foot and make an accurate throw at medium speed, chest high and over the bag (try to get in front of the ball and avoid the backhand if possible).

THE SHORTSTOP AS THE MIDDLE MAN IN THE DP

You should cover the bag on a double play when the ball is hit to the second baseman or first baseman. You might also cover on double plays that begin with the pitcher or catcher.

When the ball is hit to either the second baseman or first baseman, sprint to an area just behind second base. Using short choppy steps near the base. Place your right foot just behind the bag (almost touching) and wait for the ball to be released by the first or second baseman. When the ball is released, step across the bag with your left foot and drag your right toe over the bag.

If the ball is hit to the first baseman close to the bag, he may elect to tag the bag before throwing to the shortstop. If this happens, the first baseman should call out, "tag him!" and you would apply the tag (there would no longer be a force play after he tags first).

The Double Play

Short choppy steps will get you under control after you sprint to an area just behind the bag.

Assume a position with your right foot just behind the bag (nearly touching) and wait for the ball to be released before committing yourself across the bag.

The Double Play

When you see the ball in flight, move across the bag with your left foot as you throw and drag your right toe across the top of the bag.

THE 1-6-3 DOUBLE PLAY FROM THE PITCHER

When the pitcher or catcher starts the double play, the coverage is established before the play starts. Before the pitcher pitches he should know who is covering second on the ball hit back to him. The same person covers if the ball is chopped in front of the plate and the catcher fields the ball.

You should "round" the bag, or make a little circle, as you approach it. After this movement, you will be heading almost directly at the pitcher. Use the same technique as before and place your right foot directly behind the bag.

"Round" your approach to the bag when the pitcher or catcher starts the double play.

When the pitcher (or catcher) releases the ball, move across the bag and drag your right toe over the bag while throwing to first.

SHORTSTOPS AND DOUBLE PLAYS—POINTS TO REMEMBER

▶ Successful double plays begin with good positioning.

▶ On balls hit within two steps of the bag, you can tag the bag yourself.

▶ When you start the double play, give the second baseman a medium-speed throw that is chest height and over the bag.

▶ When taking the throw from the second baseman or the first baseman, sprint to a point three feet behind the bag, then get under control with short choppy steps.

▶ Coverage of second base on balls hit back to the pitcher should be decided before the pitch.

▶ When the pitcher or catcher starts the double play, circle the bag as you approach it.

▶ Don't force a double play on a ball that is not a double-play ball.

4
Tagging and Coverage on Steals

With a runner on first base, the possibility of a steal or a hit-and-run play always exists. Coverage is usually dictated by which side of the plate the hitter is hitting from. With a left-handed hitter at the plate, the shortstop will almost always cover second. With a right-handed hitter up, the second baseman will normally get the call. At the higher levels, these assignments are switched from hitter to hitter and even from pitch to pitch. The shortstop will give the second baseman signs on each pitch to indicate who is covering. The switches are put on so an experienced hitter can't hit the ball through the vacated position on a hit-and-run.

THE STRAIGHT STEAL

When a runner tries to steal second, there are two ways to cover the base. The first method involves positioning in front of the bag, and the second method is to straddle the bag. Most baseball people feel that the straddle method is the more efficient.

If the shortstop covers, the second baseman backs him up; the reverse is true when the second baseman covers.

When the throw arrives, place your glove in front of the bag, with the back of your hand facing the runner (to avoid injury). When the runner arrives and contact is felt, pull your glove out. Avoid reaching for the runner, the ball can easily be knocked out of the glove. All tags should be made with the glove hand to avoid injury to the bare hand.

*One tagging method involves positioning
yourself in front of the bag.*

By placing one foot on either side of the bag, you are able to tag runners out more effectively.

Tagging and Coverage on Steals

When making the tag, place your glove against the bag, with the back of your hand facing the runner; the runner will tag himself out by sliding into the glove.

THE HIT-AND-RUN PLAY

The hit-and-run play is one of the best offensive plays in baseball. If it is executed perfectly, the defense can't stop it. By switching coverage from pitch to pitch, major leaguers are able to curtail its effects somewhat. It is not necessary to do all of this switching at the lower levels. Most hitters aren't skilled enough to hit the ball through one hole or the other.

When you are called on to cover second on a steal or hit-and-run, don't break directly to the bag. Instead, move directly at the hitter for a couple of steps, and then break to the bag. This will avoid the big hole created when an infielder breaks too early or takes the direct route.

When the runner takes off for second, a double play is usually impossible. The infielders must communicate; if there is no play at second, the infielders should call, "First, first!" to avoid an unnecessary throw.

One trick used by professional players involves the infielder faking the fielding of a ground ball when the ball is hit in the air. Many times the runner, who may or may not have seen the ball hit, will keep going to second, only to be doubled off first on the pop-up or fly ball.

RUNNERS ON FIRST AND THIRD— THE DOUBLE STEAL

The shortstop becomes an important factor when a team is defensing the double steal. When the catcher throws the ball to second to throw out the base stealer, the man on third will sometimes break for the plate. The third baseman will let the shortstop or second baseman know if the runner on third breaks for the plate. The infielder will move forward, meet the ball early, and throw to the plate. If there is no break by the runner on third, the tag at second is applied as usual. Communication is the key to defensing the double steal.

5
Catching
Pop-Ups

The first thing for infielders to establish is their areas of responsibility. If there is an overall understanding on this subject, then most problems associated with catching pop-ups are eliminated.

YOUR RESPONSIBILITY

An infield pop fly is the responsibility of the infielders, and all of the infielders should go after it until one fielder calls for the ball. If you're the one calling for it, yell your head off. You don't want to be in the middle of a four way collision as the ball goes rolling into the outfield. You can also wave your arms. But be careful never to call for the ball too soon. Strong winds can take the ball right out of your area.

What happens when two or more players call for the ball at the same time? This sometimes happens near the pitcher's mound because all four areas of the infield meet here. In this case, the pitcher should call the name of the player who should get the ball.

Finally, it's up to the shortstop and second baseman to catch pop flies that go directly behind the third baseman and first baseman.

COMING IN TOWARD THE INFIELD

When you come in for a pop-up, one thing to remember is not to call for the ball too soon. Let the ball get to its highest point before calling the play. Calls made too early are usually wrong; with a little patience pop-ups can be handled as routine plays. The ball should be caught with two hands over the head.

When the ball is in the sun, use your glove to block the sun. This play should be practiced until every player on the team is comfortable with balls in the sun. This problem doesn't go away. Even major leaguers have problems with the sun. Sunglasses will help, but using the glove to block the sun is the only effective method for catching the fly ball in the sun.

Catching Pop-Ups

Catch pop-ups over your head with two hands.

Use your glove to block the sun.

GOING BACK INTO THE OUTFIELD

You should cover a lot of ground in the outfield going after "texas leaguers" or pop-ups in shallow left field. Go back as far as possible and continue to go for the ball until you hear an outfielder call you off the ball. Communication is the key here, and the outfielder must make the infielders hear him if he wants the ball. This can be a potentially dangerous play if the players don't communicate well.

Keep going back until you hear the outfielder call for the ball.

58

6
Cutoffs and Relays

Team defense wins as many games over the course of the year as pitching or hitting. Few teams at any level of baseball play what could be called excellent team defense. Playing team defense effectively means that every player on the field knows what is expected and does his job.

As the shortstop, you should coordinate all the activities on the field concerning cutoffs and relays. You must know not only your job but everyone else's too. Every player on the field has a job to do on every defensive play.

You have one of four things to do on every play:

1. **Go get the ball and throw it in.**
2. **Become a relay or cutoff man.**
3. **Cover a base.**
4. **Back up a fellow fielder or a base.**

The following defensive assignments are generally accepted as the standard for professional baseball. They were first designed by the Los Angeles Dodgers in the 1950s, or possibly earlier. Since then, several organizations in professional ball and scores of amateur coaches have adopted these assignments for their team defense.

SINGLE TO LEFT FIELD, NO ONE ON BASE

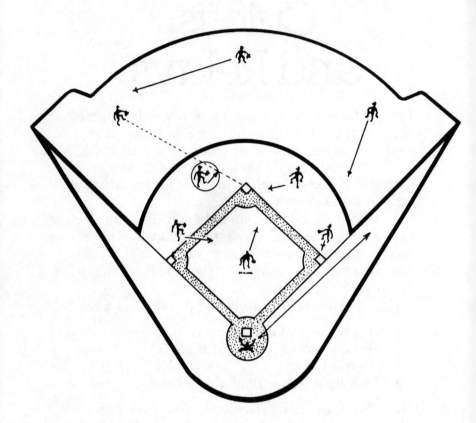

THE SHORTSTOP'S JOB

Become the cutoff man and line up ball to second base.

SINGLE TO CENTER FIELD, NO ONE ON BASE

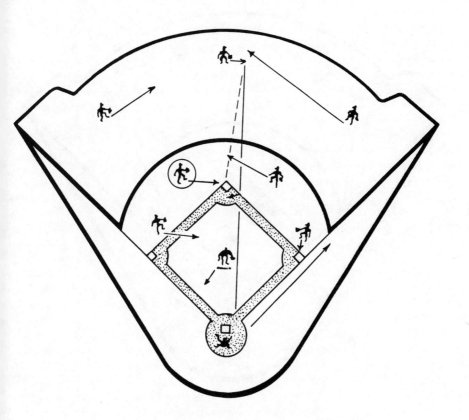

THE SHORTSTOP'S JOB

Cover second base and prepare to take the throw from the centerfielder in case runner tries to take extra base.

SINGLE TO RIGHT FIELD, NO ONE ON BASE

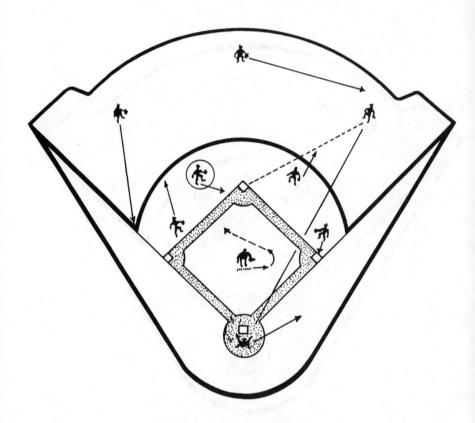

THE SHORTSTOP'S JOB

Cover second base. The throw may come to you if the runner looks like he may try to stretch it for a double.

SINGLE TO LEFT FIELD WITH RUNNER ON FIRST BASE

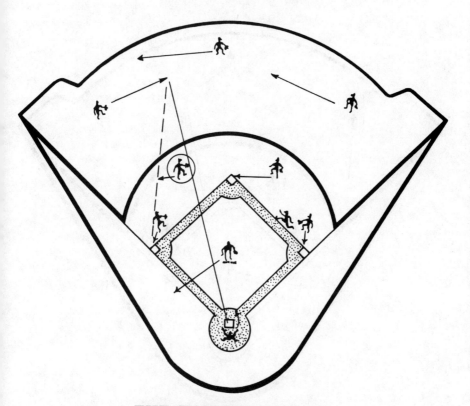

THE SHORTSTOP'S JOB

Position yourself about 45 feet from third base on direct line from third base to the outfielder fielding the ball. You're the cutoff man here, so it's your job to take the throw from the centerfielder and fire it to third.

SINGLE TO CENTER WITH RUNNER ON FIRST BASE

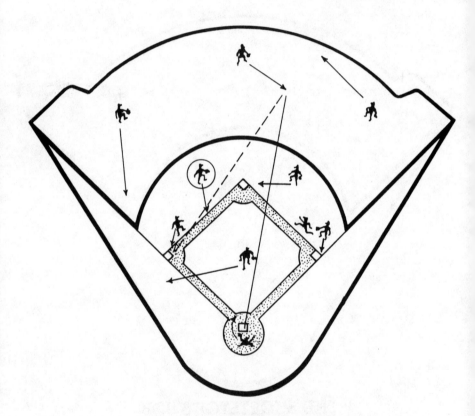

THE SHORTSTOP'S JOB

Position yourself about 45 feet from third base, on a direct line from third base to the outfielder fielding the ball. You have to make the cutoff from the centerfielder and throw to third.

SINGLE TO RIGHT FIELD WITH RUNNER ON FIRST BASE

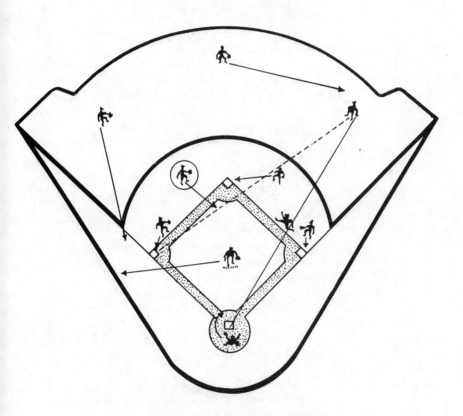

THE SHORTSTOP'S JOB

Position yourself about 45 feet from third base, on direct line from third base to the outfielder fielding the ball. You'll make the cutoff if there's a play at third.

SINGLE TO LEFT FIELD WITH RUNNER ON SECOND BASE

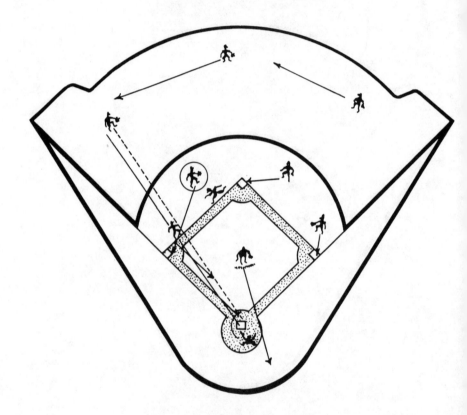

THE SHORTSTOP'S JOB

Cover third base, since the third baseman must move down the third base line to relay the ball home.

SINGLE TO CENTER FIELD WITH RUNNER ON SECOND BASE

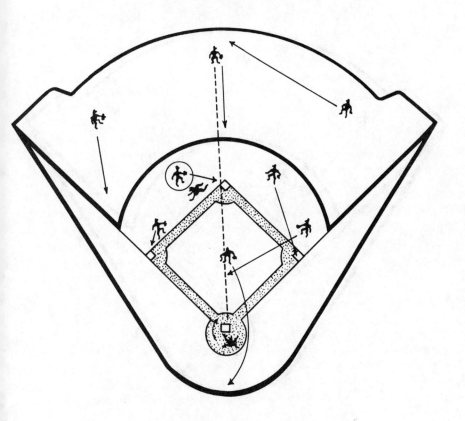

THE SHORTSTOP'S JOB

Cover second base, because the second baseman must cover first to allow the first baseman to take the cutoff from the outfield.

SINGLE TO RIGHT FIELD WITH RUNNER ON SECOND BASE

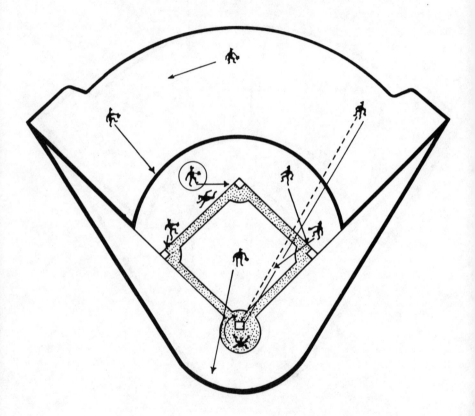

THE SHORTSTOP'S JOB

Cover second base. The throw will go home, so you probably won't be near the ball.

SURE DOUBLE DOWN LEFT-FIELD LINE, NO ONE ON BASE

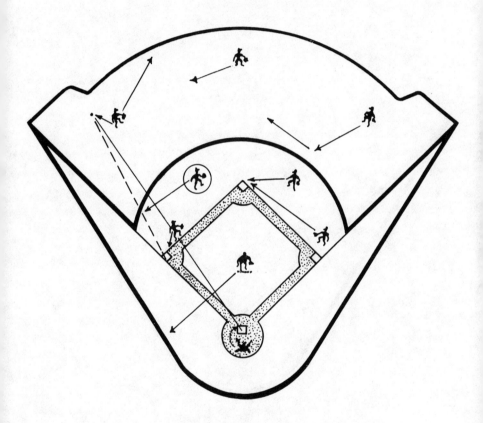

THE SHORTSTOP'S JOB

Position yourself as the cutoff man between third base and leftfielder. The throw will be to third, or to second if you can beat the runner.

69

DOUBLE TO LEFT-CENTER FIELD WITH RUNNER ON FIRST BASE

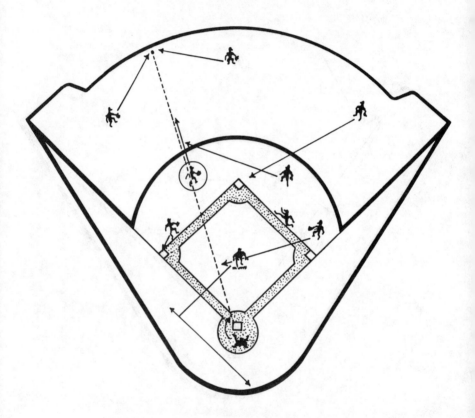

THE SHORTSTOP'S JOB

Go to left field in direct line with outfielder and plate. You'll have to make the throw home, so be ready for the throw from the leftfielder.

SURE DOUBLE DOWN RIGHT-FIELD LINE, NO ONE ON BASE

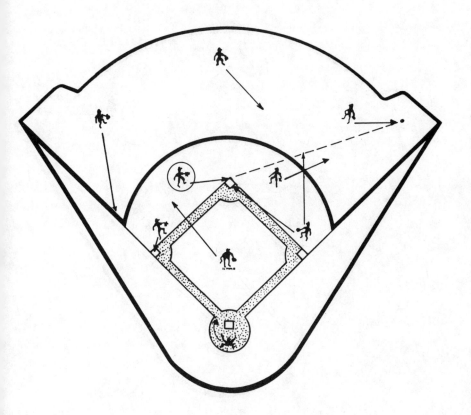

THE SHORTSTOP'S JOB

Cover second base to take the throw from the cutoff man in the outfield. It's your job to make the tag.

71

SURE DOUBLE DOWN RIGHT-FIELD LINE WITH RUNNER ON FIRST BASE

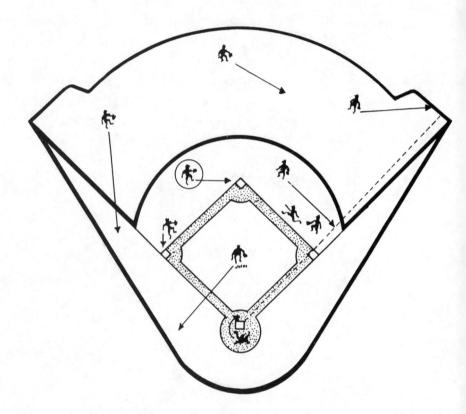

THE SHORTSTOP'S JOB

Cover second base so the second baseman can make the cutoff.

POSSIBLE TRIPLE TO LEFT-FIELD CORNER, NO ONE ON BASE

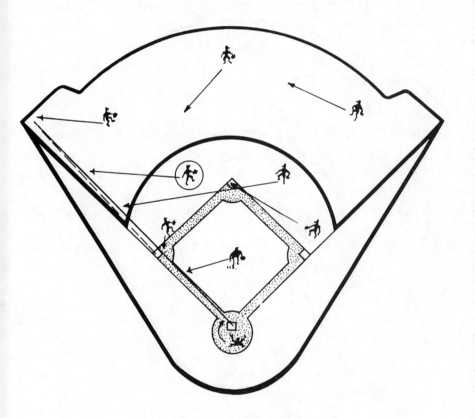

THE SHORTSTOP'S JOB

You'll be the man for the throw to third base, so move into position between third and the left-fielder along the left-field line.

POSSIBLE TRIPLE TO LEFT-CENTER FIELD WITH RUNNER ON FIRST BASE AND RUNNER SCORING

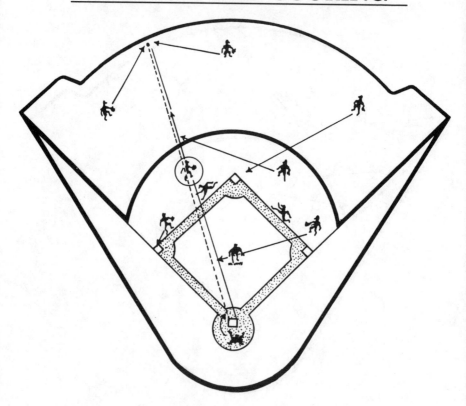

THE SHORTSTOP'S JOB

You're the cutoff man, so line yourself up between left center and the plate. When you get the ball, fire to home.

POSSIBLE TRIPLE TO RIGHT-CENTER FIELD, NO ONE ON BASE

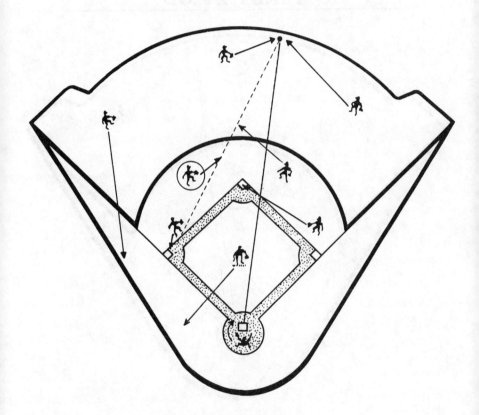

THE SHORTSTOP'S JOB

The second baseman is the cutoff man here, so your job is to back him up just in case he misses the throw. If you do get the ball, throw to third.

75

POSSIBLE TRIPLE TO RIGHT-CENTER FIELD WITH RUNNER ON FIRST BASE

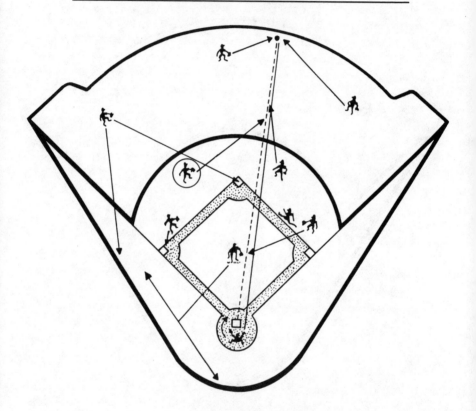

THE SHORTSTOP'S JOB

You must back up the second baseman in case he misses the throw from the outfielder. If you do get the ball, throw home.

76

POSSIBLE TRIPLE TO RIGHT-FIELD CORNER, NO ONE ON BASE

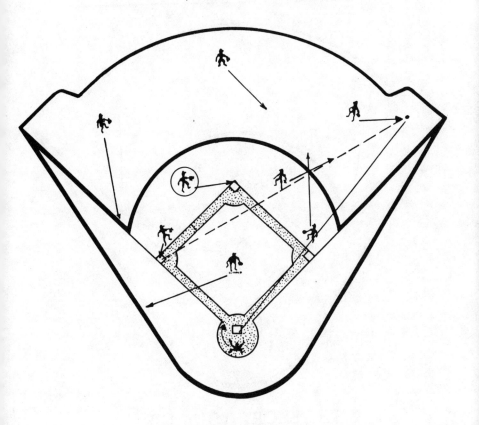

THE SHORTSTOP'S JOB

Cover second base so the second baseman can make the relay to third.

77

FOUL POP-UP DOWN RIGHT-FIELD LINE WITH RUNNERS ON FIRST AND THIRD

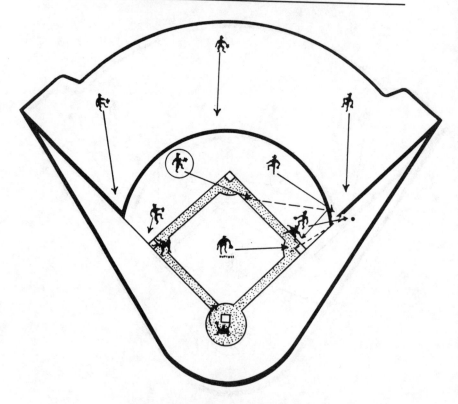

THE SHORTSTOP'S JOB

Since the runner on first will break for second if the ball is dropped, you must position yourself about 30 feet from second base to become the cutoff man and make a tag.

FOUL POP-UP NEAR FIRST-BASE DUGOUT WITH RUNNERS ON FIRST AND THIRD

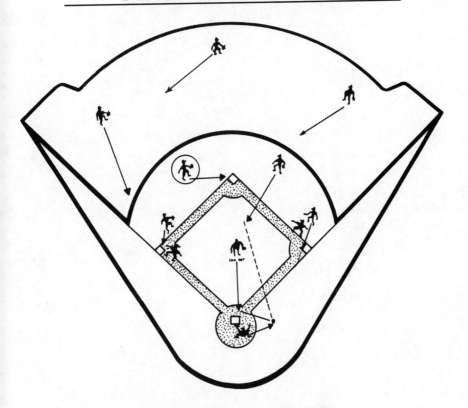

THE SHORTSTOP'S JOB

Cover second base, since the second baseman has to be near the mound to make the cutoff.

7
Rundowns, Bunt Defense, and Pickoff Plays

THE RUNDOWN PLAY

When a rundown starts anywhere on the base paths, the shortstop is always involved. You will either be a backup man or one of the two defensive players directly involved in the rundown.

A rundown develops when a runner is trapped between bases. The player with the ball is called the "charger" and the player covering the other base is called the "receiver."

As the rundown begins, the charger places the ball in his bare hand and holds it in a throwing position. His job is to make the runner commit one way or the other by running at him. When the charger reaches a point 20 feet or so from the base, he throws the ball to the receiver when the receiver says "Now!" It is not a good idea to fake throws, because the receiver is also faked out.

The man covering the base (the receiver) must first adjust to the charger (get on the same side of the baseline) as soon as possible. When the receiver says "Now!" the ball is thrown chest high and he applies the tag.

The "charger" makes the runner commit himself by running hard at him (notice the ball in the bare hand and in the throwing position).

The "receiver" says "Now!" when the charger is 20 feet from him (note that the receiver is on the same side of the baseline as the charger).

TEAM BUNT DEFENSES

There are two standard bunting situations that develop regularly. The bunt is in order with a runner on first base and no outs, and with runners on first and second and no outs and a weak hitter at the plate.

On both standard plays, the shortstop covers second base.

83

BUNT, WITH RUNNER ON FIRST BASE

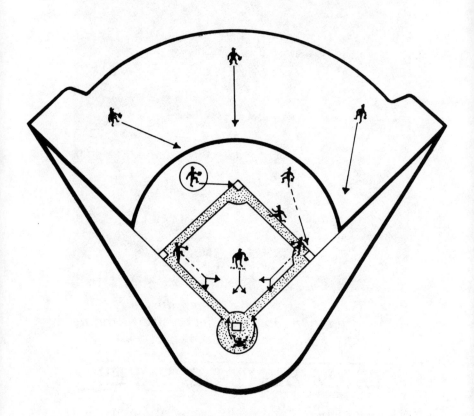

THE SHORTSTOP'S JOB

Cover second base, since the second baseman is covering first so that the first baseman can field the bunt.

84

BUNT, WITH RUNNERS ON FIRST AND SECOND

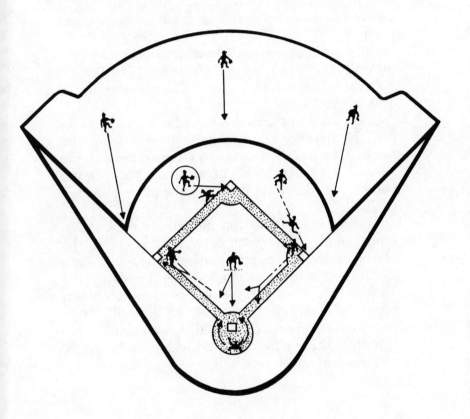

THE SHORTSTOP'S JOB

Hold the runner on second close to the bag, and cover second base.

PICKOFF PLAYS

The shortstop is very involved in trying to hold the runner close at second base. Both you and the second baseman must do a good job of bluffing in and out to prevent the runner from getting a good jump.

On occasion, you will have an opportunity to pick off a runner at second. Nothing will pick up a defense more than picking off a key runner late in a tough ball game.

One common method is called a "daylight pickoff." It involves no prearranged sign from the pitcher. In simple terms, you break behind the runner and when "daylight" (a space between the runner and the base) develops, the pitcher throws the ball.

On timed plays you and the pitcher have a sign (and usually an answer) between you before the play develops. The pitcher comes to the set position looking back at the runner. When he shows the back of his head (by looking at the plate), you break, and the pitcher counts to himself, "One-thousand-one," and turns and throws.

Both of these plays are used widely in the major leagues and youth baseball.

When "daylight" develops between the runner and the shortstop, the pitcher should spin and throw.

The timed play involves a sign from the pitcher, a response, and lots of practice between pitcher and shortstop.

TIPS FOR SERIOUS SHORTSTOPS

▶ Know your playbook well and study different game situations.
▶ When you take grounders in practice, take one play at a time and work hard on it.
▶ Practice charging the ball; it is a must at shortstop.
▶ Work on going to your right and left.
▶ Because a shortstop must throw well, take care of your arm and do everything possible to improve your accuracy and arm strength.
▶ Take lots of pop-ups in all directions.
▶ Turn all the double plays you can; this is an important play for you and your defense.
▶ The slow roller is a tough play and requires lots of practice.
▶ Know your responsibility on pickoff plays.
▶ Make sure your team's double-steal defense is airtight.

REMEMBER
The Shortstop is the Captain of the Defense.
Be a Leader, Take Charge, and be
the Most Aggressive Player on the Field.

Index

Index